"This conversation starter needs to be shared with every young woman to help her to make wise choices."

Jami Pool, MA, PLPC
counselor

"Great job! You write well and the stories are compelling."

Pam Stephens, freelance writer

"Your book is poignant and providential. It is well-balanced, personable, informative, thought-provoking, and prompt to action. It is a necessary tool."

Michelle Black,
children and youth librarian

"I read this the first time before going to bed. I awoke in the morning meditating on the many ways young women put themselves at risk and at the ways I had put myself in danger. I think the book is a great way to inspire a group of young women to share their stories, to learn from each other, and to learn about the love of God."

Marilyn Lowe, concerned mother

"[The] sense of worth [of our children and youth] is distorted by the way their marred, hyper-sexualized culture defines their value…. We can no longer afford to remain silent."

Beth Grant, author of
Courageous Compassion, p. 154

DOORS TO CLOSE, DOORS TO OPEN

Experience Genuine, Secure, Satisfying Love

by Sylvia Rivera

Dedicated to young women,
facing many attractive doors,
seeking wisdom for choices about love

Doors to Close, Doors to Open:
Experience Genuine, Secure, Satisfying Love
© 2015
Sylvia Rivera
door2close2open@gmail.com

No part of this book may be reproduced, stored in a retrieval system,
or transmitted in any form or by any means —
electronically, mechanical, photocopy, recording, or otherwise —
without prior written permission of the publisher
except in the case of brief quotations used in articles and reviews.

ISBN-13: 978-1507663868

To order this book, go to Amazon and Kindle,
Or www.doorsofhope.online

Cover art by Chris Jeanguenat (www.ebsqart.com) Used with permission.

Doors and Decisions

Which beautiful sweater to buy? Which movie to see? Which of the yummy desserts to order? Some decisions in life are relatively easy and are accompanied by laughter and fun.

Not all of life's decisions are so entertaining. Many are mysterious unknowns of much greater importance: What career do I want to pursue? Which college should I attend? Whom will I marry who is truly loving? How do I make these decisions about love?

Our decisions about love are the most challenging of all the decisions we make. They are like doors we face: mysterious, inviting, tempting, beautiful. Some may bring great love; some don't; others may seem to bring joy at first but later bring deep disappointment and pain. Appearances can be deceiving. Wisdom and discernment are needed for making decisions about love.

I've made some poor decisions in my life about love--which I'll share with you later. They led me into disappointing and dangerous places. Thankfully, with God's help, I recognized I needed to close those doors. I gained wisdom, which has brought me lasting joy, peace, and love—but I learned the painful way.

This book relates my experiences and the experiences of other women. We hope that you will become better equipped to make wise decisions about the doors that appear to lead to love.

Longing to be Loved

Loneliness and the longing to be loved are the most common and deeply-held feelings for <u>all of us</u>. Because of those emotions, we tend to do *whatever it takes* to avoid their pain. Choosing to do *whatever it takes* often means we open ourselves up to possibly unwise choices. Being "open" is considered a positive attribute in the world today; being open to whatever satisfies our own needs and longings is considered "right" and "good."

The truth is: *Complete openness makes us vulnerable to danger.* Let's take time to think about being vulnerable and the situations that can make us extra-vulnerable. <u>The most common cause of vulnerability is our hunger for love</u>.

> "Vulnerable" means to be susceptible to injury; unprotected from danger; insufficiently defended; likely to give into persuasion or temptation

Certain circumstances can make us <u>extra-vulnerable</u>: Lacking confidence and knowledge can make a person vulnerable. Openness to danger can be increased by being orphaned, or being unloved/abused by parents, or experiencing the divorce of parents, or running away from home. Poverty and illness can open us to being defenseless. Moving to a new city, or state, or country also increases our sense of helplessness because everything familiar has been left behind. The death of a close friend or family member creates a painful empty space in our hearts. Oh, the deep emotional ache! Yet opening ourselves to whatever we "feel" is the answer to our quest for love has many serious risks. We need wisdom too.

<u>Did you know that our vulnerability is visible to everyone, even when we try to cover it up with laughter or toughness?</u> When some people see our vulnerability they respond with compassion; but unfortunately others see it as an opportunity to take advantage of us and abuse us.

Think about: *What are some situations that increase people's vulnerability? Do you identify with one or more of those circumstances? Which extra-vulnerable situations are part of your life? When do you feel the most lonely or unloved or vulnerable? (For the questions asked in this book, please take time to write your answers and/or talk about them with a group of other young women who are reading this book. Blank pages for writing notes in back.)*

In this book you will read about:
- *some dangers through real life stories*
- *closing doors to protect yourselves*
- *healthy doors that truly satisfy your deepest longings for love*

My True Story

It's not easy to share my experiences of unwise decisions. I share them to warn and encourage young women. I want you to open doors of love, not of pain or abuse. I have opened doors of danger because of my own vulnerability because of loneliness, grief, ignorance, and insecurity. Those doors should have been slammed shut from the first peek behind the door.

I met a man when he showed me an apartment to rent in the new city where I had just been offered a teaching position. He asked me out for dinner and I met him at a restaurant. He ordered wine and offered it to me. I told him "No, thank you" because I would be driving home. He kept insisting. I continued to say no. A couple of weeks later he invited me to his house for dessert and a soak in the hot tub. We enjoyed talking and relaxing. I changed out of my bathing suit and into my slacks and blouse in the bathroom. When I tried to rejoin him in the living room, the door handle turned, but the door wouldn't budge. I pulled hard, again and again. I heard the doorbell ring and a woman enter the living room. I began to yell for help. The sound of their hushed voices was clear to me, although I couldn't distinguish the words. Why was I being ignored by people no more than 8 feet away from the door?! Having no cell phone, I yelled louder and louder. Eventually he unlocked the door from the hallway side. I escaped and ran out.

I met another man at a church picnic. He asked me out to dinner at a beachfront restaurant. He handed me a rose when I arrived at our table. I was so happy. Afterward we took a walk on the moonlit promenade and he kissed me. That was so romantic! Like the movies!

We started seeing one another often. I met his parents and his two little children from a former marriage. Within weeks he knelt to ask me to marry him. "Yes!" We started planning the wedding, but I began to sense that something was wrong, although I couldn't say what it was, so I prayed. Within a week I witnessed his dark side. One day in the car, he braked abruptly in rage and punched his small asthmatic son in the chest with his fist for a minor commotion in the backseat. He began being critical of me and nearly hit me more than once. I was afraid of his rage and violence, so I planned a safe way of escape with the help of a good Christian premarital counselor. I could have been harmed even more seriously in the two relationships told here.

I decided that I was unable to make wise choices about relationships because I needed to become less vulnerable before I could have a good relationship with anyone. I made a commitment to God to stop dating and to spend time learning, growing, and healing. I thank God that He helped me to close the doors of danger and to become wiser and stronger. Eventually I met a respectful, patient, tender, wise, and loving man, whom I married after two years of knowing him. We love one another more with each year together.

Think about: *What could I have done <u>earlier</u> to protect myself in the relationships shared above?*

A True Story

Sarah* drove to high school in a new Honda Accord, which her parents had given her for her 16th birthday. They also threw a party for her with their church's youth group. Her car came with a curfew and the insistence from her parents that they know where she was and who she was with at all times; they also expected her to find a job to pay the car costs.

Earlier that morning things had not started off well. Her mom had told her she must return a shirt she had bought because it was "too tight and too low." As she drove into the school parking lot, she saw her new friend Maggie wearing the exact shirt that she had been told to return. Sarah related her mom's demands. Maggie replied, "I'll give you mine tomorrow. Then you just keep it in your locker to wear at school." Maggie added that Sarah's parents were really strict and bragged about her own parents. The next day Maggie brought the shirt and another "sexy" one. "Doesn't it feel good to wear what you want to wear? You look so pretty! You're doing the right thing by following your heart," Maggie said.

Sarah confided in Maggie that she hadn't been successful in finding a job to pay for the car's expenses. "I can totally set you up," Maggie offered. "All you have to do is go out with this old guy. You'll have to kiss a little, but it won't be a big deal. I can get you money." So Sarah agreed, then arrived home before her curfew.

Please see Sources page for the information in this book.

Maggie introduced Sarah to a handsome guy named Alex. They fell in love and he became her secret boyfriend. Alex bought Sarah new clothes, perfume, music, and DVDs. Soon, they had intercourse. Sarah was convinced that he was right for her and believed her parents didn't really love her.

Sarah eventually learned that Alex ran the dating service where Maggie worked. Alex asked Sarah to move with him to Las Vegas to start their dream life together, explaining that business would be good there. One day they met in the school parking lot, where she left her car, and they drove off.

After arriving in Las Vegas Sarah suffered severe physical abuse and forced prostitution at the hands of her "boyfriend." That was just three months after meeting Maggie, who was one of Alex's prostituted women; he had demanded that Maggie lure other young women into his "business." Nearly a year later, the thin and pale Sarah escaped her enslavement when the police made a raid where she was forced to "work." She was relieved to be reunited with her parents and begin recovery.

More than 250,000 girls/youth are trafficked yearly in the USA. This dire problem was first recognized by the American government in 2000, when they passed the Trafficking Victims Protection Act to provide rights to victims rather than treating them as criminals.

Think about: *What could Sarah/her parents/the church have done or not done to reduce the chances of her being lured and then forced into what is called human trafficking, a door that appears innocent or fun at first.*

Another True Story

Theresa Flores was new in town because her father's good-paying executive position required that they move often. She was lonely, trying to make new friends at the high school. She met a guy at school and hung out with him and his friends at school for about 6 months.

One day he offered to give Theresa a ride home after school. She felt relief from having to walk home alone, but Theresa felt uneasy when he headed away from her house, explaining that he needed to get something at his house.

When the car stopped in front of his house, she stayed in her seat, waiting for him to return. He invited her to come in, but she said no. He then stuck his head in through her open window, gave her an irrepressible smile, saying, "You know, I really love you." Although uncomfortable, she walked up to the house with him.

No one else seemed to be at home. He offered her a seat and brought her a glass of soda to sip while he went to retrieve whatever he needed. The next thing she remembers is waking up in the bedroom, having been sexually assaulted. What shame consumed her! But things only got worse. A few days later her "boyfriend" showed her the photos that had been taken at his house. Then that afternoon she answered her home phone to hear an older gruff male voice warning her that the photos would be shown to her parents and that her brothers would be killed if she didn't cooperate with him. He hissed, "Be in front of your house at midnight, or else."

That was the first night of her living hell, sneaking out of her beautiful home in the suburbs in the dark to be taken places to be abused and prostituted, with multiple men in nightmarish ways. One night one of the men asked her so-called boyfriend, "What's her name?" He said, "It doesn't matter." Theresa was dehumanized, a nameless object for profit.

After two years she escaped, thanks to another job transfer for her father to a new location. Theresa left town without telling anyone where she was going. Those phone calls in the middle of the night were to a number that was no longer in service. Theresa Flores wrote a book called *Slave Across the Street: Blackmailed into Sex Trafficking*, and she travels around the United States to warn young women of the danger that lurks in ordinary American communities. She declares that she recovered from her living nightmare through counseling together with Jesus' love and healing.

<u>Although Sarah's and Theresa's stories ended with freedom, most of the girls/youth taken into human trafficking never escape.</u>

Think about: *Why was Theresa vulnerable? What could she have done to protect herself?*

Doors of Love

We all want love, but what is it? Warm affection, concern, kindness, goodness, patience, humility, unselfishness, honesty, protection, trustworthiness, faithfulness, honor, respect, and value--those words all sum up the definition of love found in the Bible. When we compare ourselves or others to that list, we see that none of us loves perfectly or is loved perfectly. Even still in our pursuit of love, *we can learn to discern* when someone appears to like us yet is dangerous because of selfishness, unkindness, dishonesty, control issues, greed, and disrespect. *Sometimes we overlook those things because we want to believe that we are loved when in fact we aren't.* We should not settle for less than what we are worth!

<u>We are precious, beautifully made, truly lovable women, with the image of God imprinted on our very souls!</u> *Often when we are vulnerable, we turn off our discernment and values, and are blind to what we know isn't for our good.*

We need to choose to be ourselves, the women God created us to be! We can pray for God to bring us into healthy relationships. We can take time, a long time, at least a year, to get to know someone before we allow our hearts and souls to grow too close. Then still, wise steps are needed. We can be willing and courageous to say, "No, thank you" or "I'm outta here" when we need to close a door. <u>Remember: You are truly worth protecting!</u>

Doors of Danger

When we first meet someone, a door opens up just a crack, and then more widely as the relationship is developed over time. We need to assess if what we see or hear just behind that door from the very beginning is safe or possibly dangerous to us emotionally and physically, perhaps foretelling probable abuse. We need to close dangerous doors as early as possible.

Often we don't recognize the serious evil around us. York Moore, who is concerned about the vulnerability of youth, says: "In our day, evil has been romanticized, relegated to the status of myth and portrayed for us as hard-bodied, happy, teenaged vampires. But the myth is all too real as modern-day vampires prey on the flesh of young girls...drinking their youth and absorbing their souls in the brothels [places of prostitution] where countless are lost."

Our God-given consciences can be dulled, silenced, and hardened
- By listening only to what our culture says is "OK"
- By being emotionally vulnerable and not saying "no"
- By rebelling against or ignoring what we know is actually for our good

We need courage and healthy support to shut doors of danger when our consciences warn us.

Think about: *Who in your life is wise, mature, and trustworthy to support you as you make decisions about love?*

Prepare to Face Doors

WHAT COULD BE THE DANGERS IN THESE SITUATIONS?

- Detailed instructions on how to become a better, more loveable, sexy woman through makeup, diet, exercise, hair, dress, etc.

- Frequent putdowns and criticisms

- "Falling in love" and becoming engaged right away

- Meeting a stranger online

- Meeting a stranger while at the mall or at Starbuck's

- Alcoholic drinks, or drinks that may be drugged

- Intense insistence about what the person wants

- Guided imagery, relaxation techniques, hypnosis

- Disrespect of your faith, or family, or friends

- Isolated places, such as an empty apartment, hot tub, moonlit beach, etc.

- Expensive romantic gifts

- Generous gifts from a girlfriend who wants you to meet a guy she knows; going on blind dates

- Requests to keep things secret

- A person pretends to hit you, or actually hits you

- An invitation for any kind of sexual activity, or being forced into it

- Offers for modeling jobs

- Job offers for a great paying job somewhere else, not locally

Think about: *Seriously consider each situation and its potential dangers, then make a specific plan of action to protect yourself rather than being vulnerable. Every plan for each possible danger may be stated like this:*

Knowing that _____

can be dangerous, I choose to_____

The Perfect Door of Love

God designed us to be in good, healthy relationships with Himself as well as with others. As we pray and study the Bible's teachings, He will lead us and teach us about good, nourishing relationships. Even still human love is limited. *Even the people we most admire can never completely satisfy our need for love.*

Our yearning for love is like a deep Jesus-shaped hole in our soul. We will still be hungry in the deepest part of ourselves, even with a wonderful relationship—*until* we open the Perfect Door of Love, which is a personal, intimate, growing, and transforming relationship with Jesus Christ! I'm not talking about religion but *a relationship*.

We often assume that God is somehow insufficient because we can't see or touch Him. *Sometimes it takes making foolish choices by opening doors wherein lies danger before we are ready to call out to God for help, rescue, and wisdom.*

When we seek God and close dangerous doors, we find out that God is more than enough. His wisdom is good and perfect, and He points us to doors of genuine human love. He is Truth. He helps us understand that the world is full of deceptive doors that can lead us to destruction. He hears and answers our sincere prayers with what is truly best for each one of us.

God's love far exceeds any human ability to love and satisfies our deepest needs. He will never abandon or reject us like some people do. Only God perfectly forgives, loves, accepts, approves, and accompanies us. Jesus showed us the ultimate form of love by dying and being raised to life again so that we could be free to choose a peaceful and satisfying relationship with God—Father, Son, and Holy Spirit—the Answer for all we want, need, and imagine!

Think about:

If you <u>don't have a relationship with Jesus</u>, would you like to begin a relationship with Jesus the Son of God? <u>Even if you've opened many dangerous doors already</u>, He's here now ready to listen as you invite Him to come into your heart and give you a new life full of love! Simply talk to Him with an open heart and He will begin to transform your life as you follow Him!

If you have a relationship with Jesus, would you like to <u>deepen your relationship with Jesus</u>? What can you do to grow closer to Him? Hint: Time together—sharing and knowing one another—builds loving relationships. How do you do that with Jesus?

SOURCES

True Story
Sarah's story is found in a book by Nita Belles, *In Our Backyard.* (Self-published, 2011 [ISBN 978-1-61215-797-9]), pp. 4-22; all names changed; more true stories.

Current statistics in an inspiring book by Beth Grant, *Courageous Compassion: Confronting Social Injustice God's Way* (Springfield, MO: My Healthy Church), pp. 13, 153, 154.

Another True Story
To learn more about Theresa Flores, get her book; also go to YouTube for "Human Trafficking: A Survivor's Story" by HLN.

Doors of Love
Read some of the wonderful Bible verses about love—
I Corinthians 13:4-7; Romans 5:8, 12:3,10; 13:10; Philippians 2:3; Psalm 139:13-16; Genesis 1:27.

Doors of Danger
R. York Moore, *Making All Things New* (Downers Grove, IL: IVP Books, 2012), p. 43.

The Perfect Door of Love
Some biblical examples of women who were vulnerable and found the Perfect Door of Love include—
> *Ruth and Naomi:* read Ruth, chapters 1-4
> *Woman at the well*: read John, chapter 4
> *Woman caught in adultery*: read John, chapter 8: 1-11

When I say I am a Christian
I'm not shouting "I am saved"
I'm whispering "I got lost!"
"That is why I chose this way."
When I say..."I am a Christian"
I don't speak of this with pride.
I'm confessing that I stumble
and need someone to be my guide.
When I say..."I am a Christian"
I'm not trying to be strong.
I'm professing that I'm weak
and pray for strength to carry on.
When I say..."I am a Christian"
I'm not bragging of success.
I'm admitting I have failed
and cannot ever pay the debt.
When I say..."I am a Christian"
I'm not claiming to be perfect,
my flaws are too visible
but God believes I'm worth it.
When I say..."I am a Christian"
I still feel the sting of pain
I have my share of heartaches
which is why I seek His name.
When I say..."I am a Christian"
I do not wish to judge.
I have no authority.
I only know I'm loved. *Author unknown*

**Call the anti-trafficking hotline if you or someone you know
is being exploited or is at risk.
1-888-3737-888
Text, the same number, *be free***

NOTES

NOTES

NOTES

NOTES

NOTES

NOTES

Made in the USA
Columbia, SC
11 October 2022